Original title:
Through the Fern's Eyes

Copyright © 2025 Creative Arts Management OÜ
All rights reserved.

Author: Sebastian Whitmore
ISBN HARDBACK: 978-1-80581-810-6
ISBN PAPERBACK: 978-1-80581-337-8
ISBN EBOOK: 978-1-80581-810-6

The Watchful Earth

In the shade, the clovers hide,
While ants march on, full of pride.
A squirrel sneezes, makes a scene,
Nature giggles, all serene.

The daisies dance, they sway and lean,
Each wave a laugh, a playful sheen.
The clouds overhead roll in a jest,
Making shadows, they never rest.

Nature's Quiet Witness

A butterfly lands with a flirty spin,
Her dance and twirl, a secret grin.
The puddles ripple with a snicker,
As frogs debate who's the quicker.

A lizard lounges, sun on back,
Watching the world on its lazy track.
With every rustle, a chuckle shared,
In the green realm, all joys declared.

A Silent Chorus of Foliage

Leaves rustle softly, a whispered joke,
While branches giggle, and roots provoke.
The thorns hold gossip, sharp yet bright,
As petals flutter in sheer delight.

In the thicket, secrets play abound,
With critters scurrying, laughter crowned.
Every rustle, a tale to weave,
In nature's arms, who wouldn't believe?

Fronds of Insight

Fronds stretch out, waving hello,
With gentle nudges, they steal the show.
A breeze comes in, a ticklish tease,
Turning whispers into giggling trees.

The sun peeks in, a cheeky ray,
Illuminating mischief at play.
From roots to tips, the fun ascends,
In this green world, the laughter never ends.

The Stillness of Shadows

In the forest, shadows dance,
A squirrel pauses for a glance.
Whispers tickle, leaves all quirk,
As branches play their hidden work.

The sunlight bends, a playful tease,
While critters conspire with eager ease.
Laughter rustles in the breeze,
As laughter ripples through the trees.

Nature's Silent Narrator

A beetle rolls a tiny stone,
Comparing lives with those alone.
Crickets chuckle, frogs do croak,
As trees bear witness, never woke.

A cheeky bird, it sings a rhyme,
Confusing rhythms, mismatched time.
The woeful owl just shakes its head,
While nature giggles, ever led.

Gazing from the Ground

From lowly earth, the critters peek,
With curious creaks and sounds unique.
A gopher mumbles, "What a scene!"
While daisies argue over green.

The grasshoppers leap with a laugh,
Comparing heights in their own craft.
"Bet you can't jump as far as me!"
"Challenge accepted, just wait and see!"

Kaleidoscope of the Forest

Colors burst in the leafy maze,
As butterflies prance in a dizzying blaze.
A raccoon jests, "Look at my style!"
While nearby flowers giggle for a while.

Sunlit spots become the stage,
Where playful echoes engage.
Nature quips in every hue,
Reminding us to laugh anew.

The Lens of the Wild

A squirrel stole my sandwich,
With flair, he made his run,
Diving under leafy greens,
That little thief's such fun!

The rabbits hold a meeting,
With carrots as their snacks,
They gossip 'bout the hawks above,
And dodge all nature's hacks.

A turtle dons his glasses,
Says fashion is the key,
But moves so slow on Sunday,
You'd think he's lost at sea.

The birds, they hit the disco,
With chirps and flapping wings,
They dance atop the branches,
While the frog just awkwardly swings.

Secrets Within the Thicket

A hedgehog found a hedgehog,
A mirror in the night,
They winked and shared their secrets,
A prickly friendship's plight.

The raccoon with his bandit mask,
Raids every picnic there,
While laughing at the humans,
Who don't see him near the chair.

The owl with his old glasses,
Says wisdom's just a joke,
When he hoots an owl riddle,
Even trees begin to choke!

The fireflies are the party,
With lights from here to there,
But one flew right into my pie,
And buzzed without a care.

Hidden Narratives of Nature

The ants are busy writers,
Plotting through the ground,
They pen a tale of biscuits,
And hope they won't be found.

A bee's a honey merchant,
With deals, it flies around,
But stings if you won't buy from him,
And buzzes very loud.

A fox tells tales of wonder,
To snakes who listen close,
He claims he saw a lion,
But he's just a boastful ghost.

The trees are great performers,
With rustles in the breeze,
But when they try to dance,
They simply drop their leaves.

Lowly Perspectives

A snail won every race,
On a slow and slippery track,
He grinned with all his slime,
While the rest all fell right back.

The beetle bumps a party,
With tiny, bug-like beats,
He rolls his disco ball,
While munching on some treats.

The worm dreams of the skies,
While wriggling in the dirt,
He wants to join the eagles,
But fears a total spurt.

And when the mice all gather,
For tiny tales at night,
They hope the cheese won't vanish,
Or they'll scurry in a fright.

Reflections From Nature's Outskirts

In the shade where creatures tease,
A squirrel mocks the bending trees.
Leaves giggle as the breezes play,
Nature's jesters on display.

Bugs in hats, the toads decree,
"Hop along, join our jubilee!"
The sunbeams wink, all is absurd,
Nature's laughter is unheard.

Veiled Perspectives of the Greenery

Mossy carpets dance with grace,
Frogs in shoes, a funny face.
The ants parade on tiny trails,
With whispers of mischievous tales.

Wobbling bees in dizzy flight,
Chasing dreams in morning light.
Petals flap like comedy,
Petty pranks in harmony.

The Subtle Lens of the Forest

Owls in glasses, reading lore,
A raccoon chef cooking s'mores.
Mushrooms giggle in their spots,
Tickling ferns in silly knots.

Breezes gossip, secrets told,
Among the woods, so brave, so bold.
Trees sway gently, swaying right,
Nature's punchlines take to flight.

Veins of Green

The ivy laughs at old stone walls,
While dandelions host their balls.
Nutty acorns roll and spin,
Nature's party, let's dive in!

Lizards strike a pose and freeze,
Caterpillars ride the breeze.
Giggling winds whoosh and twirl,
What a wild, wacky world!

Eyes of Wonder

Frogs with glasses, what a view,
Pointing out the world askew.
Bright-eyed bugs on swing sets fly,
Buzzing tales that fill the sky.

The sun peeks through a leafy grin,
Inviting everyone to join in.
Nature's humor never ends,
In the woods, we're all good friends.

Eyes of the Understory

In shadows deep, the critters play,
A squirrel's dance in the leaf buffet.
Mice chatter gossip, a cheeky crew,
While ants march on, as if they knew.

The mushrooms chuckle, a spritely band,
With hats so tall, they take a stand.
Toadstools whisper secrets to the ground,
As giggles echo all around.

Observations of Clover and Cedar

Beneath the cedar, clovers giggle,
Tickling roots with tiny wiggles.
A snail in a hurry, what a sight!
He's late to the party, all in fright.

The cedar shakes with laughter loud,
As bugs discuss being part of the crowd.
Squirrels argue over acorn delight,
While beetles roll logs, oh what a night!

Lattice of Leaves

A leaf just swayed, with a soft little grin,
As whispers of wind twirled its kin.
"Watch out for the rain!" shouted a sprout,
While daisies danced, without a doubt.

The leaves all plotted a prank below,
To drop a raindrop on a wandering toe.
"Surprise!" they shouted with a rustle and shake,
Nature's laughter, a fun little quake!

Nature's Lens of Observation

With acorn caps, the critters spy,
On ants who march a workday by.
A ladybug sights a prize on a leaf,
And dances around, quite beyond belief.

Frogs croak jokes with a ribbiting twist,
As breezes pass by, they can't resist.
The sun winks down at the playful crew,
Nature's camera clicks, and laughter is due!

A World Enclosed in Green

In a forest bright, where critters dance,
Frogs wear crowns, so take a chance.
Squirrels gossip, tails in a flurry,
While rabbits plot a grand old curry.

Mossy carpets, a soft, cushy bed,
A tree stump throne for the squirrel's head.
Acorns drop like royalty's gems,
Nutty parties, with wig-wearing stems.

Leaves whisper secrets, gossip made loud,
A raccoon's mask, he's so very proud.
Jaybirds arguing, who's the best singer?
While the worm's showing off a new slinger.

Every corner, a strange little sight,
Crickets playing tunes in the night.
A world enclosed, filled with sweet laughter,
Nature's jesters bring joy ever after.

Gazing upon the Quiet Kingdom

Upon a throne made of twigs and leaves,
The king of bugs, in sunlight weaves.
He holds court with ants in parade,
While a snail takes its sweet time to invade.

Butterflies request a dance in the sun,
"Whose wings are bigger? It's all just fun!"
The grasshoppers cheer, jump to delight,
As the ladybug juggles, in mid-flight.

A dance-off erupts, who will take the crown?
With spins and flips, the bug world frowns.
But wait! A spider spins a web of cheer,
Catching laughter, we all give a cheer.

Nestled in whispers, a realm full of jest,
Every leaf holds a giggle, a jest.
Time stands still, in this green delight,
In a kingdom quiet, but never contrite.

Stories Woven in Sylvan Hues

Beneath a tree, where shadows blend,
Chirping tales, the critters send.
Mice write novels with tiny quills,
As frogs discuss their epic thrills.

A fox in glasses reads with great flair,
Teaches young raccoons to share and care.
Tales of whispers from the wind's breath,
Each story shared brings a giggle, not death.

In the root's embrace, laughter resides,
With beetles as lawyers, no one hides.
Their courtroom antics, a laugh-a-minute,
Encouraging rabbits to try and commit.

Over branches, yarns of joy are spun,
Each twist of fate, a quirky run.
Bright hues in laughter, the woods are alive,
Where stories woven help the heart thrive.

The Silent Watcher of the Woods

In the hush of trees, a watcher grins,
An owl's perch, where the fun begins.
With eyes so wide, the nighttime see,
He chuckles at antics, like mice in a spree.

Branches sway, as whispers grow loud,
Dancing shadows form a giggling crowd.
The silent sage of the leafy dome,
Watches the forest turn into a home.

A fox darts past, slipping on dew,
While crickets cheer for the brave of crew.
The owl holds its hoot, bemused and sly,
As fireflies flaunt their glow in the sky.

All night long, a watchful gaze,
Through laughter and light, the forest plays.
In the quiet realm, joy floats on high,
With the silent watcher's approving eye.

In Lush Corners of the Earth

In corners green, where shadows play,
The critters think it's time for tea.
A squirrel dons a tiny hat,
While rabbits twirl in jubilee.

With mushrooms stacked in silly rows,
They dance and spin, no care in sight.
A snail's on stage, it's time to pose,
Then slips, oh what a woeful plight!

The hedgehog brings a beanbag chair,
To judge the moves with tiny paws.
The woodland laughs without a care,
While nature takes a round of applause.

In every nook, a giggle sings,
As nature's folly rules the day.
In leafy realms, the party swings,
As sunlight melts the frowns away.

Beneath the Arching Fronds

Beneath the fronds where shadows creep,
A frog rehearses for the show.
It jumps and flips, oh what a leap,
And lands right in a patch of slow.

The lizards laugh, they can't contain,
As bugs provide a raucous cheer.
The frog just grins, it feels no pain,
Next time, it thinks, I'll stick to beer.

A sloth chimes in, "What's all the fuss?"
While munching leaves, it hums a tune.
The dance floor shakes, it's quite a plus,
As night descends and stars commune.

With critters joined in playful jest,
Each leafy bough contains a joke.
Together, they all know the best,
Is laughter shared beneath the cloak.

Whispers in the Glade

In the glade where secrets flow,
A rabbit wears its Sunday best.
It curtsies low to say hello,
And trips, of course, a tiny jest.

The trees all chuckle, branches sway,
At tales exchanged by mossy stone.
A wise old owl wants to convey,
That fashion faux pas should be shone.

A ladybug with polka dots,
Becomes the gossip queen tonight.
With wings a-flutter, it plots a lot,
To snag the stars, a daring flight.

As whispers swirl like autumn leaves,
The sacred glade becomes a show.
With bioluminescent thieves,
A sparkle-party starts to glow.

Gaze Beneath the Green Canopy

Gaze beneath the canopy,
Where things are bright and quirks abound.
A raccoon wears a monocle,
It claims to be the smartest round.

The vines all sway with playful glee,
While ants discuss the latest news.
A snail with style sips herbal tea,
In this affair, there are no blues.

The sunlight splashes all around,
A mockingbird sings silly tunes.
The forest floor feels quite renowned,
As laughter dances with the runes.

So come and join this jolly spree,
Where ferns partake in fun and cheer.
Oh, what a sight, come take a peek,
The woodland life is quite sincere.

Seeing with the Shadows

In a dance of light, they prance,
Leaves giggle, holding hands.
Squirrels chase their own tall tales,
Beneath the growth, there are little trails.

Mushrooms wear their little hats,
Who knew fungi could throw such spats?
A wise old owl, playing chess,
Says logic's best in this leafy mess.

Rabbits play hide-and-seek,
They hop around, no need to peek.
With shadows laughing in the sun,
Nature's game has just begun.

Creatures giggle in a spree,
In this woodland jubilee.
Clad in greens, a funny sight,
Forest life, pure delight!

The Forest's Quiet Muse

Moss-covered stones hold laughter tight,
Whispers echo in the night.
A hedgehog wearing tiny shoes,
Is always up to share some news.

A squirrel with a funky bow,
Dances by the plants aglow.
While butterflies take waltzing turns,
The forest hums and quietly churns.

Fluffy clouds pass overhead,
The trees nod, 'Aren't we fed?'
With nature's brush, it paints a grin,
For every loss, there's always win.

A gnome with dreams, how very rare,
Sips from puddles without a care.
Under twinkling stars, they share,
The funny things that linger there.

Underneath the Canopy's Gaze

Rustling leaves hold secrets tight,
With spindly fingers, they invite.
A grasshopper on a leaf,
Croons a song, beyond belief.

Beneath the arch of leafy hands,
A cricket starts a marching band.
The tree trunks sway with perfect grace,
As if they're keeping up the pace.

Ladybugs don polka dots,
Sipping dew from tiny pots.
With giggles high and laughter sweet,
A carnival of tail and feet.

Chasing shadows, bouncing light,
Every critter takes to flight.
In this world, where whimsy reigns,
Joy wins out, and laughter gains.

Botanical Whispers

In gardens lush, where gnomes reside,
Petals laugh, they cannot hide.
A daisy winks, a tulip bows,
At nature's fun, it takes a vow.

Caterpillars throw a ball,
While butterflies flutter, heed the call.
Grapes compete in a grapevine race,
Smiles abound in this leafy space.

Witty vines twist on a dare,
Juggling berries, up in the air.
While dragonflies spin wild tales,
Their laughter dances on the trails.

Lilies splash water in jest,
Knowing blooms can never rest.
In nature's laughter, joy aligns,
Amidst the beauty, humor shines!

Secrets of the Woodland Gaze

In the thicket, whispers abound,
Squirrels plot with leaps and bounds.
Mice gossip 'neath the big oak tree,
Who knew the woods had such a spree?

A rabbit winks with a twitchy nose,
While the hedgehog's dreaming of toast and scone.
Foxes wearing fashionable coats,
Strut their stuff in the woods they roam.

The mushrooms dance in polka-dot joy,
While the owls hoot, 'Who's my favorite boy?'
Nature's antics, quite the delight,
In this woodland, laughter takes flight.

So sit back, enjoy this lively stage,
Where woodland creatures act their age.
With furry friends that laugh and play,
Secrets flourish in a fanciful way.

Silhouettes in the Dappled Light

Bouncing shadows on the forest floor,
A rabbit leaps, oh, what a score!
The sunbeams play hide and seek with cheer,
While deer giggle, 'Oh, do come near!'

A fox, slick and sly, strikes a pose,
Wearing shades, as coolness flows.
The raccoons chime in with their chatter,
What's important? Food, it's all that matters!

The butterflies flutter in sheer delight,
Performing pirouettes in the fading light.
And far-off, a toad croaks a tune,
Under the watch of a cheeky raccoon.

Laughter echoes amid the trees,
Where woodland creatures dance with ease.
Silhouetted stories come to light,
In this playful woodland night.

Echoes of the Forest Floor

Crunch and rustle, what's that sound?
Bunnies hop, they're lost and found.
Leaves whisper secrets, soft and sly,
As the chipmunks giggle, 'Oh my, oh my!'

A squirrel's stash of acorns galore,
Tells the tale of a hoarding score.
With tiny hands, he counts in glee,
While birds tweet, 'How rich shall he be?'

The shadows tease in a playful jest,
As the hedgehog curls up for a rest.
'Front-row seat to this woodland lore,'
Laughs the mouse, peeking out of his door.

These echoes dance through mossy halls,
And nature's laughter in twilight calls.
Whimsical whispers stir the air,
In this green realm, without a care.

The Intimate Silence of Green

In a world where quiet reigns supreme,
A frog croaks out a silly dream.
The trees stand still, but oh, what fun,
When laughter bubbles up like the sun!

Beetles march in their little parade,
While snails are late, yet unafraid.
The silence fills with chuckles bright,
As shadows play in pure delight.

The chipmunk squeaks, 'Can you keep a secret?'
While the owl hoots, 'I sure could use a ticket!'
Nature's comedy, a silly scene,
In the intimate silence, of vibrant green.

So take a breath, and join the cheer,
In this woodland realm, where all's sincere.
With every quiet grin and grin,
The forest shares its laughter within.

The Cool Gaze of Greenery

In the shade, the leaves do sway,
Teasing bugs that come to play.
They laugh as raindrops start to fall,
While soaking up the sun's bright call.

A squirrel pops in, all in a rush,
Trying to hide from the playful hush.
With a wink and a leafy grin,
The ferns just giggle, let the fun begin!

Chasing after shadows, so sly and spry,
A dance of light as the day goes by.
Frogs croak tunes from their soggy thrones,
While the shy blooms blush in subtle tones.

So here we are, in this leafy dome,
Where laughter grows and wild things roam.
If you listen close, you'll hear their cheer,
Nature's jesters, always near!

Lurking in the Light

Beneath the beams where sunlight plays,
Little critters spin their ways.
A ladybug struts with flair and glee,
While teasing shadows just wait and see.

The ferns, a stage for this mad parade,
Like green comedians, they won't fade.
With every rustle, a punchline's born,
As squirrels declare their battlehorn!

Caterpillars wiggle, ants march on cue,
In nature's casino, there's plenty to do.
Betting on which leaf will dance or twirl,
They chuckle and spin in a leafy whirl.

So when you wander, stop for a peek,
Join in the fun, laughter's the key!
For ferns might just wink and give a shout,
In this world of green, there's no doubt!

Fronded Observations

With a stretch and a yawn, the sun arises,
Ferns unfold whispers, share their surprises.
They watch the blooms flaunt their bright hues,
While snickering softly at the bees' endless blues.

A turtle meanders with a silly frown,
Wearing a shell like a clumsy crown.
The leaves snicker as he takes his time,
Conversations hidden in nature's rhyme.

The wind gets cheeky, gives a playful shove,
Causing all flowers to giggle and love.
Ferns nod along to the breezy jest,
In this merry woods, they feel so blessed.

They see us wander, with blunders galore,
And throw subtle jabs while we explore.
With every glimmer in the sun's warm glow,
Life's a chuckle when the ferns put on a show!

Nature's Subtle Glimpses

Among the thickets, a tricky spy,
With leaves that chat and branches high.
The riddle of roots that twist and twine,
Tickles the earth with a giggly sign.

A rabbit hops with floppy ears,
While ferns point fingers; oh, the cheers!
They whisper stories of days gone past,
In this quiet corner, fun unsurpassed.

The wind joins in, twirling like a pro,
A leaf-edited dance that puts on a show.
Amidst the laughter of crawling things,
The cerulean sky above gently sings.

So take a stroll where the wild things play,
Listen closely to what they say.
For in this green realm of nature's play,
Every glance is a wink, come what may!

The Garden's Avid Watcher

In the garden, something stirs,
A snail in shades of green confers.
With tiny binoculars in hand,
It claims to be the smartest in the land.

The flowers gossip, petals shake,
They argue over who's the fake.
The bee just buzzes, rolls its eyes,
While ladybugs don their wise guy ties.

The worms all laugh, they wriggle with glee,
At the thoughts of grass so fancy and free.
"I'm the ruler!" squeaks the loudest ant,
While thorns just grumble, "You can't recant."

So the garden hums with quirky tales,
As every critter dreams and wails.
Life's no soap opera, we might agree,
In this rowdy plot of green comedy.

Eyes in the Underbrush

Under leaves, the world awakes,
Where secrets thrive and laughter shakes.
A hedgehog snickers, winks with pride,
With a dandelion as its guide.

The bushes shake, there's quite a ruckus,
A squirrel claims it's just pure luck us.
With acorns thrown and playful jibes,
The undergrowth is full of vibes.

Caterpillars plan a waltz so grand,
While crickets play in a funky band.
"Oh look, a shoe! Shall we try it on?"
They scramble forth until it's gone.

And when the moonlight starts to glow,
The world beneath begins to show.
With antics wild and jokes so spry,
The underbrush is where we fly.

The Nature of Perception

A beetle thinks he's quite a sight,
In spectacles that are not quite right.
He struts along with dazzling flair,
While the tulips just stare and swear.

The gopher's digging seems offbeat,
Dancing while he looks for a treat.
Hummingbirds hum a quirky tune,
As shadows leap beneath the moon.

A rock sits still, feeling neglected,
Yearning for stories, but unselected.
"Can't you see my wisdom not worn?"
He mumbles softly, feeling forlorn.

Yet perceptions shift with every glance,
In nature's stage, there's just a chance.
To laugh and tumble, share a jest,
For even stones can dream and zest.

Botanical Reflections

Amidst the blooms, they all convene,
While flowers giggle, how very keen.
"Who wore that color?" one leaf inquires,
While mockingbirds tell tales of choiring choirs.

The daisies sway with every tease,
As pastels flaunt their blooming ease.
A sunbeam dances, flowers twirl,
Creating chaos in this leafy whirl.

Cacti grimace, declaring they're tough,
But burst into laughter, it's all in good fluff.
"Fashion statement? It's just my spikes!"
They smile as the wind adds its likes.

In this botanical playroom bright,
Every petal laughs into the night.
Reflection shows what nature can be,
A riot of joy, wild and free.

Unveiling Nature's Lens

A critter peeks from leafy home,
With little thoughts of where to roam.
It dreams of cheese and crumbly pie,
While watching clouds go strolling by.

Morning dew on blades that dance,
A nature show, a silly prance.
The squirrel wears a tiny hat,
Looking sharp, imagine that!

A ladybug in polka dots,
Plays tag with ants in silly spots.
The world's a stage, the fronds the seats,
For all the giggly, silly feats.

As shadows cast a playful jest,
The ferns just laugh; they're truly blessed.
Nature's crew in leafy play,
Oh, what a joy to live this way!

Beneath the Tranquil Fronds

In green nooks, a worm does squirm,
Confused by light, it's quite a term.
Opening meetings with the roots,
It charms the beetles in their boots.

A butterfly with style galore,
Lands on a leaf to sing and soar.
It's not a horse, but dreams of flight,
Chasing raindrops, oh what a sight!

The cricket beats a boisterous tune,
While frogs in chorus croak in June.
They shake their legs, they dash and hop,
Each getting ready for the crop!

Amidst the fronds, giggles abound,
A secret world that's joyfully found.
With every rustle and swish of green,
Life blooms in laughter, sweet and keen.

Soft Sighs of the Underbrush

In thickets wild, a toad does snooze,
While dreaming of adventure's muse.
He jumps to greet a passing breeze,
Waving to bugs with charming ease.

A band of mice have formed a line,
Chasing shadows, feel so divine!
With tiny hats and shoes of fluff,
They dance around, it's all quite tough!

A snail in style, so slow and bright,
Carries a shell in sheer delight.
It shells out wisdom, quite absurd,
While sharing tales that seem unheard.

The grasshoppers hop with playful ease,
As laughter drifts upon the breeze.
In quiet corners, tales entwine,
Nature's capers, simply divine!

A Whispered Viewpoint

Hiding low, a chipmunk grins,
Charting paths for silly wins.
With food tucked in cheeks, so chubby,
He races friends, each one a buddy.

Underneath the leafy shroud,
Ants march by, so fierce and proud.
They carry crumbs much larger still,
While making plans for their next meal.

A mischief aimed at the old tree,
Where squirrels plot in glee, oh, see!
They toss twigs in a game divine,
Nature's players, they'll be just fine!

As sunlight spills on the soft terrain,
They laugh in joy, not a hint of pain.
With whispered secrets, as days blend,
Oh, what a world! The fun won't end!

The Green Wisdom

In the garden, toe-to-toe,
A snail shared secrets with a crow,
"Why rush?" the mollusk said with glee,
"Life's a race, but not for me!"

The daisies giggled, swaying bright,
While ants held meetings day and night,
Their tiny suits and grand charades,
Made even slugs throw leafy parades!

A wise old oak dropped its acorn,
Whispering tales of times long gone,
"Grow slow, my friends, don't be so grim,
Life's a joke; enjoy the whim!"

So if you wander by the plot,
Remember it's not what you've got,
But laughter shared beneath the sun,
A leafy realm where jokes are spun!

Underneath the Leafy Veil

Underneath the leafy shade,
A cricket chirped, his jokes well-made,
"Why did the leaf refuse to dance?"
"It's not my style; I prefer to prance!"

Nearby, a beetle donned a hat,
Claiming he was really a diplomat,
With every step, the dirt did swirl,
"Let's negotiate!" he gave a twirl.

A ladybug rolled her eyes wide,
"Come on, dear friends, let's take a ride!"
The ants brought snacks, the worms played tunes,
Under the sun, beneath the moons.

With giggles echoing all around,
The woodland creatures gathered 'round,
They knew life's short, a whimsical spree,
In the leafy veil, they felt so free!

Eavesdropping on the Wilderness

In the bush, I took my spot,
Eavesdropping on the chatter, hot!
A frog declared he'd win a race,
While squirrels scoffed, all in their place.

An owl hooted, wise and slow,
"Let's not forget about the show!
When dusk arrives, I'll lead the night,
With stories sure to bring delight!"

The bushes rustled, laughter soared,
A dance-off challenge was then roared,
With twirls and jumps, the critters leapt,
In the wild, sweet dreams were kept.

Each whispered tale, each jesting cheer,
Brought all the woodland folk so near,
In secret corners, joy does abide,
With nature's humor as their guide!

The Sway of the Green World

The grass swayed like a dancer bold,
With tiny feet and hearts of gold,
A worm declared, "I'm off to prance!"
"The earth is my stage!"—oh, what a chance!

Butterflies fluttered in a race,
Chasing their shadows in a chase,
"Catch me if you can!" they teased with glee,
As petals chuckled beneath the tree.

Mushrooms popped up like splats of paint,
"Who's the artist?" asked a saint,
"Nature's the muse, let's have some fun,
Creating joy 'til the day is done!"

With every wiggle, every spin,
The green world giggled under its skin,
For in each leaf and every vine,
A funny tale waits, oh so divine!

The Perspective of Petals

Petals dance in the breeze,
Giggles floating with ease.
Sunlight shines on their cheer,
Petals whisper, 'Come near!'

Butterflies play hide and seek,
With each flutter, they peak.
Laughing at the beetle's woe,
As it tumbles, oh so slow!

Raindrops tickle the ground,
Rippling laughter all around.
Flowers roll in bright delight,
Poking fun at clouds in flight.

In this garden, joy spills out,
Making sure there's no doubt.
Life's a joke in every hue,
That's the perspective anew!

Dwelling in the Green Shades

In the shadows, critters peek,
Each one has a funny streak.
Squirrels playing on the grass,
Waving to the snails that pass.

Mice are plotting in their lair,
Cheese experiments to spare.
With a giggle and a squeak,
It's laughter they both seek!

The tall weeds gossip and chat,
While frogs croak, 'Did you hear that?'
Shady laughter fills the air,
Breezy jokes everywhere!

Dwellers dance in leafy rooms,
Creating life amid the blooms.
In green shades, hilarity reigns,
Where funny quirks are no strain!

Undergrowth Revelations

In the underbrush, secrets thrive,
Buggies thrive, they come alive.
Crickets chirp a comic tune,
As worms wiggle in monsoon.

Mushrooms chat about the rain,
Poking fun at trees in vain.
Lizards lounge, got no cares,
Trading laughs without a glare.

Nutty acorns share their tales,
Of ups and downs and silly fails.
Silly antics in the dark,
Just look—there's a snoring lark!

Underneath this leafy dome,
Each creature finds a home.
Revelations bubble to the light,
With every chuckle, pure delight!

The Grass's Observant Eye

The grass just laughs at the sky,
Watching clouds drift and pry.
'Hey, look at that ship up there!'
It says while swaying with flair.

Bugs are dancing a wild jig,
Life's a party; it's all big!
Ants march by with a funny style,
Making sure to tread a mile.

Tall blades whisper secrets low,
Sharing jokes only they know.
Every footstep, a new refrain,
Makes the ground chuckle again.

In this field, no room for strife,
Laughter blossoms, full of life.
The grass rolls its eyes up high,
What a wacky world nearby!

The Soft Breath of the Wilderness

In the woods where whispers play,
Tiny treasures hide away.
Squirrels gossip, branches shake,
Mossy carpets, nature's spake.

A snail in haste, what a view!
Slipping past, in a meeting queue.
The shy raccoon craves a snack,
Late-night raids, and then a lack.

Breezes hum a silly tune,
While owls giggle at the moon.
The wildflowers wear silly hats,
Conspiring with the acrobatic bats.

And if a fern joined the choir,
It'd laugh and jump, never tire.
In this realm where antics meet,
Nature's stage plays can't be beat.

Witnessing Time in the Understory

In a shady nook, time stands still,
Ferns gaze up, what a thrill!
They chuckle at the ants so small,
Marching like they own it all.

A butterfly does wobbly dives,
With all the grace of blundering hives.
Amidst the ferns, they giggle wide,
As beetles join on a silly ride.

Clouds drift by, in lazy spins,
Taunting lightly, playful whirs and grins.
Down below, the roots discuss,
Who's had the wildest day, thus?

Ah, the laughter from the ground,
Nature's jesters all around.
In this space, so rich with cheer,
Time lets loose, nothing to fear.

The Realm Beneath Sunlight

Dancing shadows on the floor,
Where ferns prance, oh what a score!
Tiny critters play hide and seek,
Whispered secrets, no need to speak.

Sunbeams tickle leaves with glee,
While caterpillars share their tea.
A ladybug's funny sprawl,
On a fern, she feels so tall.

Crickets joke with toads in glee,
Nature's jest is pure esprit.
Try to catch their banter quick,
But it's all a charming trick.

A world where laughter holds the sway,
Under the sun, both night and day.
Come along, join this delight,
In the ferns, life's a bright sight!

Hidden Narratives of the Ferns

In deep green realms where jokes unfold,
The ferns weave tales, both shy and bold.
With secret smiles, they share their lore,
Of fuzzy things that scamper and soar.

A gnome once danced with a leaf so spry,
Claiming the wind taught him how to fly.
Mushrooms wink in their little spots,
Thinking they know all the fun plots.

And as the shadows flicker and sway,
Ferns spin yarns of a fierce ballet.
With snappy quips like leaves in a breeze,
They giggle at quarrels of buzzing bees.

Nestled beneath canopies wide,
In every layer, joy can't hide.
So lean in close, lend them your ear,
For the ferns tell tales full of cheer.

Patterns Woven in Shade

In dappled light we dance around,
Little critters lost but found.
Fluffy tails and tiny squeaks,
Nature's jest in leafy peaks.

Stripes and spots, what a show!
Silly antics all aglow.
Mossy rugs for footloose feet,
While mushrooms hum a funky beat.

A shadow here, a shadow there,
Watch out! A beetle with flair!
It twirls and spins, a daring feat,
Making everyone laugh in the heat.

With giggles caught in leaf-clad arms,
Nature's whimsy works its charms.
Underneath the woodland's gaze,
Life's a joke in lush displays.

Observing Life from the Fern's Nest

Perched aloft on blades of green,
I spy the world, a quirky scene.
Squirrels gossiping in high cheer,
While ants parade, no hint of fear.

A rabbit hops with wiggly nose,
Chasing butterflies in lovely prose.
They giggle softly, swift and sly,
Like tiny jesters in the sky.

The breeze whispers tales of woe,
Of garden gnomes that stand in tow.
With painted hats and painted grins,
They keep the secrets of our sins.

I sit and chuckle from my throne,
As critters frolic, porch-like stone.
In this green realm, they rule the jest,
Nature's circus, truly blessed.

In the Embrace of Verdant Whispers

Draped in greens, a secret chat,
A squirrel sings, a sudden spat.
Leaves bobbing, whispers in the breeze,
While owls blink and the sun does tease.

Flowers giggle, standing tall,
Tickled by raindrops, they sway and sprawl.
Bees buzz tunes, but oh what rhymes,
As they plot those sticky crimes!

A grumpy toad looks quite bemused,
At ladybugs, so brightly bruised.
They've painted spots in red and black,
Flaunting colors—they'll never lack.

What fun unfolds in verdant space,
With every glance, a silly face.
Laughter echoes through the grove,
In these woods, joy's the trove.

Quiet Observations in the Glade

In quiet corners, jokes unfold,
Where mushrooms sprout and tales are told.
A hedgehog rolls, a prickly ball,
With giggles and snorts, he has a ball.

Beneath the stars, fireflies wink,
A secret dance, they swirl and blink.
As crickets chirp their nightly song,
In this glade, we all belong.

A wise old owl with spectacles tight,
Watches the world, oh what a sight!
With wisdom draped in feathered guise,
He rolls his eyes at foolish tries.

Laughter lingers in the night air,
As creatures gather without a care.
In this haven, joy ignites,
A funny tale under moonlit lights.

Nature's Lenses Unveiled

In the forest's playful cheer,
Tiny creatures buzz and sneer.
A snail wears shades, what a sight!
His slow-motion stroll is pure delight.

A chipmunk juggles acorns in glee,
While the owl just hoots, 'That's not for me!'
Squirrels on branches, a circus act,
Performing stunts, oh what a fact!

The daisies gossip, petals in a throng,
'Who wore it better, me or that prong?'
Nature laughs softly, a ticklish tone,
In this wild world, we're never alone.

With colors bursting in every view,
The woodland humor shines right through.
Miracles blend where the laughter's found,
In this green stage, joy knows no bound.

In the Heart of the Fronds

Beneath the leaves, a ticklish dance,
Where ants in formation prance.
A ladybug dons her best attire,
While toasters toast by the campfire!

The rabbits are plotting a grand buffet,
'Carrots for you and greens for me, hooray!'
Mice in tuxedos, all dressed for tea,
Invite the frogs for a symphony.

Breezes chuckle, leaves start to play,
A melody that makes the trees sway.
Each branch a stage, each root a joke,
Nature's comedy, a riotous cloak!

In cozy shadows, life's a jest,
All creatures gather, they're truly blessed.
With laughter sewn into the very roots,
The forest is alive, full of funny hoots!

A Gaze Amidst the Underbrush

In the thicket, a porcupine wears shades,
While snickering squirrels swap funny trades.
A hedgehog's face is quite the tease,
He argues with grass, 'I'm not your squeeze!'

The bushes murmur, secrets unfold,
A chattering chat at the break of cold.
Crickets chirp a rhythmic song,
'Did you hear that joke? It won't be long!'

Butterflies flaunt their wings on a breeze,
Leading ants on a dance, oh what a tease!
The grasshoppers nod, keep the pace,
While a dandelion puffs out in grace.

Nature's antics are fresh and bright,
Every creature sparkles in joyous light.
With laughter echoing rich and bold,
The woods, a theater, stories told.

The Dance of Leaf and Light

In sunlit glades, shadows play tricks,
Where a worm in a bowtie pulls off some kicks.
A gust shimmies through, like a sly conman,
While the sun chuckles, 'Catch me if you can!'

Dancing mushrooms would steal the show,
A polka party, let the good vibes flow!
The frogs croon softly in playful cheer,
'Join in the fun, lend us your ear!'

With rustling leaves, the trees shake their heads,
'Not another joke about our threads!'
But giggles spill from the blooming ground,
Where plants whisper secrets, humor unbound.

Each moment a jest, how life entwines,
In every corner, joy brightly shines.
In this verdant realm, laughter's the light,
The dance of nature is truly a sight!

Secrets of the Woodland

In the woods where squirrels plot,
Each acorn's worth a whole lot.
Wise old owls make little sense,
They hoot and laugh at past events.

Frogs leap out with grand surprise,
In tiny suits and bowler ties.
They croak about their big, bold dreams,
Sipping dew from silver streams.

Mice gather round, they take a vote,
Should we wear hats, or coats, or both?
Chasing tails in silly runs,
Woodland laughter never shuns.

And when the sun begins to fade,
They dance like crazy in the glade.
Secrets shared among the trees,
In their world, it's all a breeze!

Shadows in the Bracken

Beneath the leaves, a rabbit spies,
A shadow dances, oh what a surprise!
With long ears flipped, it hops around,
Giggling softly, not making a sound.

In bracken beds where critters meet,
A hedgehog rolls, unsteady on its feet.
Just watch the way those snails compete,
To slide along that mossy seat!

Bats zoom by, all in a whirl,
Squeaking jokes, they twist and twirl.
The night is filled with silly sights,
Where shadows turn into giggly flights.

Oh, the fun beneath the moon,
Where every critter sings a tune.
In bracken's shade, they laugh and play,
Making every night a holiday!

Lush Hues of Unseen Perspectives

In vibrant greens and yellows bright,
Tiny bugs have quite the flight.
They zoom around with zig-zag flair,
Swapping secrets in the air.

A ponderous snail, slow but wise,
Wears a crown made of leaves that rise.
As he glides on soft, green moss,
He shares tales of his great loss.

Frogs with sunglasses take a lie,
Claiming to reach the sky so high.
But when they leap, they miss the mark,
And land right back, a merry lark!

Blades of grass, a makeshift stage,
Where critters act in their own wage.
From flowers' hues—a funny view,
In lush perspectives, all feels new!

The Silent Watcher

A wise old tree stands oh so still,
With bark like wisdom and roots that thrill.
It watches birds with chatter bright,
And squirrels who jest till the fall of night.

The breeze brings whispers, a secret song,
Of clumsy creatures that can't get along.
The tree just chuckles, its limbs doing a dance,
For every mishap is a chance for a prance.

In shadows lurking, the watcher spies,
A raccoon's antics, a master of disguise.
With sticky paws and a crown of leaves,
It steals some snacks; oh how it deceives!

Yet all is well in the woodland's heart,
As laughter echoes, a joyful art.
The tree will keep all secrets tight,
For in this world, all wrong feels right!

Whispers Beneath the Canopy

In meetings held by tree and stump,
The squirrels share their latest jump.
A rabbit's tale of lost sweet carrots,
Makes even the stoutest badger laugh like parrots.

The owls gossip in the night,
About who stole the last moonlight.
A gopher's joke, so absurdly deep,
Makes the bark beetle laugh till they sleep.

In the shade where shadows dance,
The breeze gives all a chance to prance.
Even the mushrooms wear happy grins,
As ants parade in tiny chins.

Beneath the boughs, a giggle flows,
Nature's humor always shows.
With leafy smiles on every sprout,
Laughter's echo holds no doubt.

Glimpses of a Hidden World

Beneath the leaves, a raccoon spies,
On wandering worms and bright blue flies.
A hedgehog's cap made of pine cone,
Leaves little doubt he loves to moan.

The fireflies wink, a dazzling crew,
As frogs croak tunes they always knew.
A beetle's car, too loud for the night,
Makes every critter jump, what a fright!

With each glimpse of the hidden ways,
Creatures laugh in the sun's soft rays.
A turtle's slow pace, but sharp as a dart,
Teaches everyone the fun of heart.

Fungi giggle, their spores in the air,
While foxes show off their playful flair.
Life's silly dance is never discreet,
In this world, every day is sweet.

The Green Veil's Secrets

Behind green veils, secrets unfold,
As chipmunks argue who's braver, who's bold.
The chattering birds on branches so high,
Share tales of romance with the shy passersby.

In mossy corners, whispers arise,
About raccoons wearing clever disguises.
The toads tell stories of magical streams,
Of pranks played on snoozing sunbeams.

Each leaf has a chuckle, a sigh of delight,
While shadows paint laughter under the light.
Frolicsome sprites with laughter so bright,
Play tricks on the gnomes, oh what a sight!

And when the sun dips below the green,
The night brings giggles, a silly scene.
The forest knows how to throw a good jest,
With laughter blooming, it's truly the best.

Shimmering Shadows of the Forest

In shimmering shadows, secrets play,
As squirrels compete in a nut relay.
Fireflies twinkle with mischief around,
While the laughter of owls shapes the sound.

Each rustle and trample brings giggles anew,
The dance of the leaves adds a funny view.
A raccoon fiddles with a lost shoe,
While rabbits applaud, what a hilarious crew!

In the dusk's embrace, the creatures collide,
With skittering tales their joy can't hide.
Fungi poke fun at the shy, sleepy moose,
As the whole forest joins in, what a ruse!

The shimmering shadows hold a party tonight,
With grins from the brambles and giggles in flight.
Every critter is ready to put on a show,
In the land of the silly, where laughter will grow.

Nature's Hidden Gaze

In the woods where critters play,
A squirrel steals lunch like it's okay.
He checks left, he checks right,
With a little acorn tight.

The bees dance like they own the place,
Buzzing about with peculiar grace.
A flower watches, shaking her head,
While wishing for some peace instead.

The mushrooms laugh in a snickering tone,
As butterflies argue over a cone.
Each petal gossips, a juicy tale,
While the fox rolls by in a stylish veil.

Tree trunks whisper secrets so sly,
As the wind carries giggles that fly.
In this lively, lush, green spree,
Nature's quite the comedian, don't you see?

The Earth's Observant Eye

Rabbits hop in their own parade,
Wearing hats that they've handmade.
They wiggle and twist, what a sight!
Flaunting their style, oh what delight!

The clouds peek down, they chuckle so loud,
At the ants forming a tiny crowd.
Cartwheeling leaves swirl around,
As flowers shrug, "Hey, what's that sound?"

A tortoise snickers as he takes a nap,
While the sun plays tricks—what a clever chap!
Shadows stretch and dance, they prance,
While toads look on, unsure to chance.

Fungi whisper beneath their breath,
"Did you hear the jokes? They dance with death!"
Nature's humor hides in plain sight,
A comedy act both day and night.

Green Glories of the Ground

Grass blades gossip, a green brigade,
Whispering tales of daylight's parade.
Each dew drop sparkles with wisdom rare,
While the snails discuss fashion with flair.

The rocks are grumpy, stuck in their wedgie,
As the caterpillar shows off his edgy.
He wriggles and jiggles, a grand debut,
While the daisies sigh, 'We wish we could too.'

A brook babbles on, witty and bright,
"Heads up, folks, I'm outta sight!"
With a splash and a dash, he speeds on by,
Frogs jump on board, they wave goodbye.

So if you walk in nature's embrace,
Watch for the wonders that keep up the pace.
For laughter awaits in each little nook,
Just ask the trees, they'll share their book!

In the Embrace of the Foliage

Under the leaves, where shadows mix,
A raccoon learns some new party tricks.
He tumbles and rolls, what a funny sight,
While fireflies giggle, lighting the night.

Moss makes a carpet, plush and so lush,
As the hedgehog stumbles in a rush.
"Oops, pardon me!" he grumbles with glee,
As the ferns all chuckle, "You're still a cutie."

Butterflies flutter, they're in a debate,
Who's more graceful, who's just first-rate?
While the toad croaks out, "Let's settle this now!"
With a splish and a splash, he takes a bow.

In this lively dome of green delight,
Every creature's welcome, day or night.
So give a cheer for the whimsy around,
For nature's the best, funniest ground.

A Thicket of Thoughts

In a thicket of tangled dreams,
Laughter bubbles like flowing streams.
Whispers dance within the leaves,
Where nonsense wears a crown that weaves.

The squirrels plot their nutty scheme,
While mushrooms burst in a comical gleam.
Every breeze carries a giggle,
Nature's jesters doing a wiggle.

I saw a rabbit trip on a root,
Falling down in a furry suit.
It laughed, oh what a silly sight,
In the thicket, all feels bright!

With each rustle, a secret unfolds,
In the green, every tale holds.
So let's chuckle at life's own strife,
In this patch of whimsical life.

The Underside of Harmony

Underneath the leafy shroud,
Worms groove like they're in a crowd.
The toads croak in a playful beat,
While the ants march with silly feet.

Each raindrop lands in a comical way,
Causing puddles where critters play.
All insects join the vibrant rave,
In harmony, no one's a knave.

The sun winks down on this funny crew,
As butterflies dance in skies so blue.
With every flutter, a chuckle shared,
In this wild world, nobody's scared.

What joy lies in nature's embrace,
Every creature finds its place.
Together in laughter, let's abide,
In the green where giggles reside.

In the Stillness of the Green

In the calm of the sunlit glade,
Laughter floats, never to fade.
A gopher pops up, looks around,
And then promptly falls back to the ground.

The flowers giggle, oh so sweet,
As bees buzz by, tapping their feet.
Windchimes giggle with clinks and clinks,
While the grass holds its breath and winks.

Each shadow dances, a playful waltz,
Nature's toys come with no faults.
Lively fungi in polka dots,
Bring joy to all, thanks a lot!

In the green, smiles never cease,
Every leaf whispers its own peace.
Join the fun, share a cheeky cheer,
In this stillness, laughter draws near.

A Fern's Quiet Chronicle

Once upon a time in lush green,
Lived a fern with a thought unseen.
It peeked at the world with a grin,
As other plants felt quiet within.

A caterpillar wobbled by,
Wearing stripes and a joyful tie.
"Look at me!" it proclaimed with pride,
The fern chuckled, "Oh, what a ride!"

Under moonlight, shadows pranced,
Even quiet leaves had a chance.
A cricket jumped, missed its cue,
While the fern whispered, "What'll you do?"

With every breeze, a chuckle floats,
In the hush, unexpected anecdotes.
A fern's tale is filled with jest,
In a quiet world, it loves the best.

www.ingramcontent.com/pod-product-compliance
Lightning Source LLC
Chambersburg PA
CBHW070320120526
44590CB00017B/2754